William Battles
The Anger Squiggles

An Anger-Management Program For Grades 3-6

WRITTEN BY
Katherine MacLeod, MSW

ILLUSTRATED BY
Jeffrey Zwartjes

I would like to extend a special thank you to Renata Chase, LCSW, for being the inspiration behind this book and for teaching me to be the social worker that I am today.

William Battles The Anger Squiggles

10-DIGIT ISBN: 1-57543-157-2
13-DIGIT ISBN: 978-1-57543-157-4

COPYRIGHT © 2008 MAR*CO PRODUCTS, INC
Published by mar*co products, inc.
1443 Old York Road
Warminster, PA 18974
1-800-448-2197
www.marcoproducts.com

PRINTED IN THE U.S.A.

Table Of Contents

Introduction

William Battles The Anger Squiggles is an effective tool for teaching anger-management and assertiveness skills. Its use of age-appropriate metaphors and terminology enables students to truly understand the concept of anger. Students who learn the curriculum will be able to clearly explain how people lose control of their anger and describe different ways to prevent this from happening. They'll become acquainted with assertiveness skills and other tools specifically designed to help rid them of their angry feelings. You may use this book in its entirety or divide the content into parts that address specific needs. Designed primarily for small-group instruction, this curriculum is also appropriate for use in whole-class lessons.

How To Use
William Battles The Anger Squiggles

William Battles The Anger Squiggles may be used in a variety of ways. The program includes:

▷ *William Battles The Anger Squiggles*, a storybook you may use independently and read to students. Each page includes text and an illustration. If you're using the storybook as an independent activity, you may wish to reproduce it, color each illustration, laminate the pages, and bind them into a book. You may also use this storybook as part of the anger-management program.

▷ The reproducible student version of *William Battles The Anger Squiggles* may be used with the adult storybook or with the anger-management program. It includes the same illustrations as the adult version, but abbreviated text. As the leader reads his/her version of the story, students can follow along with the booklet. Students may color the pictures in the booklet and keep their booklets for their personal libraries. The student version is also a component of the complete anger-management program, in which certain pages are presented to students during each session.

▷ Both the storybook and the student version may be utilized in a whole-class setting. Many of the activities listed in the small-group curriculum are also appropriate for use with an entire class.

▷ The *Anger-Management Group Curriculum* is a 10-week small-group counseling program that emphasizes anger-management techniques through topics included in both the leader's storybook and the student version of *William Battles The Anger Squiggles*. The curriculum is designed for groups of 4–8 students in Grades 3–6. Each session lasts about 40–45 minutes.

▷ The curriculum may be utilized in three different ways. You may use it in its entirety, teaching children about anger management as well as assertiveness. Or you may divide it into two parts: using Sessions 1–6 to teach anger management and Sessions 7–10 for assertiveness training.

ASCA National Standards For
William Battles The Anger Squiggles

PERSONAL/SOCIAL DEVELOPMENT

Standard A: Students will acquire the knowledge, attitudes and interpersonal skills to help them understand and respect self and others.

PS:A1   Acquire Self-Knowledge
PS:A1.1   Develop positive attitudes toward self as a unique and worthy person
PS:A1.2   Identify values, attitudes and beliefs
PS:A1.5   Identify and express feelings
PS:A1.6   Distinguish between appropriate and inappropriate behavior
PS:A1.8   Understand the need for self-control and how to practice
PS:A1.9   Demonstrate cooperative behavior in groups
PS:A1.10   Identify personal strengths and assets

PS:A2   Acquire Interpersonal Skills
PS:A2.2   Respect alternative points of view
PS:A2.6   Use effective communications skills
PS:A2.7   Know that communication Involves speaking, listening, and nonverbal behavior
PS:A2.8   Learn how to make and keep friends

Standard B: Students will make decisions, set goals and take necessary action to achieve goals.

PS:B1   Self-Knowledge Application
PS:B1.1   Use a decision-making and problem-solving model
PS:B1.2   Understand consequences of decisions and choices
PS:B1.3   Identify alternative solutions to a problem
PS:B1.4   Develop effective coping skills for dealing with problems
PS:B1.6   Know how to apply conflict resolution skills
PS:B1.10   Identify alternative ways of achieving goals

Standard C: Students will understand safety and survival skills.

PS:C1   Acquire Personal Safety Skills
PS:C1.7   Apply effective problem-solving and decision-making skills to make safe and healthy choices
PS:C1.10   Learn techniques for managing stress and conflict
PS:C1.11   Learn coping skills for managing life events

William Battles The Anger Squiggles

Leader's Guide

Allow me to introduce William. He's an average kid, with average friends, who goes to an average school, and usually has pretty average days. But today will be different. Today will be anything but an average day.

What could possibly happen to William, you ask? Let me tell you: Today William will **EXPLODE**. No, no, no, William won't literally explode, but he sure will lose his temper. I mean "red-faced, fist clenched, yelling, crying, smoke coming out of his ears, doing things he wouldn't normally do" losing his temper.

What is the cause of this blow-up? Something so small that on an average day, William wouldn't give it a second thought. But we already know that today won't be like most days for William. We know that today will be different. So here is what finally pushed William over the edge: Peter Duncan cut in front of him in line at the drinking fountain.

Yes, you heard correctly. While William was patiently standing in line, Peter muscled his way to the front. What happened next shocked even William. His fists clenched into tight balls. His face felt hot and turned tomato red. William's hands developed a mind of their own and threw Peter to the ground. William heard himself scream, **"Get out of my way!"** He stormed away, but the principal's whistle stopped him in his tracks. Mr. Ortega had seen it all.

William Battles The Anger Squiggles © 2008 Mar✳co Products, Inc. 1.800.448.2197

Knowing what kind of morning William had might help you understand what caused him to explode. In order to explain fully, I need to tell you about Anger Squiggles. Yes, Anger Squiggles ... Squiggles that grow and fill us up whenever we get angry. These Squiggles are perfectly normal and don't usually cause us too many problems. But there are days when those Anger Squiggles get out of control. Do you know what happens then? Yes, you guessed it: We **EXPLODE**! Just like William did.

Now back to our story: What happened earlier in the day that caused Anger Squiggles to take control of William? Hmmm ... Where do I begin? Might as well start first thing in the morning, when William was awakened not by his alarm clock but by his teenage sister yelling, "You're late, Silly Willy!" William hates being called "Silly Willy" and before he knew it, he had a short, fat Anger Squiggle inside of him. Scary? Wrong! One little Anger Squiggle is no big deal.

But as you have probably guessed, the story doesn't end here. Let's take a quick look at William's morning so we can get back to him at the drinking fountain. After his rude awakening by Big Sis, William faced one frustrating situation after another. He missed breakfast and, instead of his favorite Sugary Snaps, William had dry toast. That brought one long, skinny Anger Squiggle into the picture.

In his dash to catch the bus, William left his homework on the kitchen table. Bing! Bing! A spiky, red-headed Anger Squiggle appeared as a result of that tragedy.

15

When William finally got on the bus, he discovered that the only seat left was between two girls from Grade 5. The rest of the kids on the bus hooted, whistled, and teased him. Because of that humiliation, a striped, fanged, hideous-looking Anger Squiggle and a brown, lumpy, three-horned Anger Squiggle grew inside William.

Can anyone tell me what was happening here? Yep, you guessed it. William was filling up with Anger Squiggles. There was hardly any room left in that body of his. If one more annoying thing happened, another Anger Squiggle would try to squeeze its way in, causing William to **EXPLODE**!

William Battles The Anger Squiggles © 2008 Mar∗co Products, Inc. 1.800.448.2197

Let's get back to William as he patiently waits in line to use the drinking fountain. Remember: He has had a rotten day, and many different Anger Squiggles are swimming around inside him.

Now, unknown to Peter, the tiny Anger Squiggle that arrived when he cut into line in front of William was what we call *the straw that broke the camel's back*. That tiny Anger Squiggle would normally cause no problems for William. But William was already filled with Anger Squiggles, so it had nowhere to go, and the other rotten Squiggles began to leak out to make room for it.

When Anger Squiggles start to leak out of our bodies, they do so in different ways.

What do you think happens when Anger Squiggles leak out our eyes? You're right: **We cry.**

What about when Anger Squiggles leak out our mouths? Exactly! **We say bad words or things we might feel bad about later.**

20

Can you imagine what happens when Anger Squiggles leak out our hands? Yes! **We might push, shove, hit, or throw things.**

How about through our feet? Absolutely! **We might kick or run away.**

21

Some Anger Squiggles like to leak into heads and tummies. Instead of causing you to hit, kick, or yell, these Squiggles cause you to feel really bad, giving you a headache or stomachache. Sometimes both at the same time!

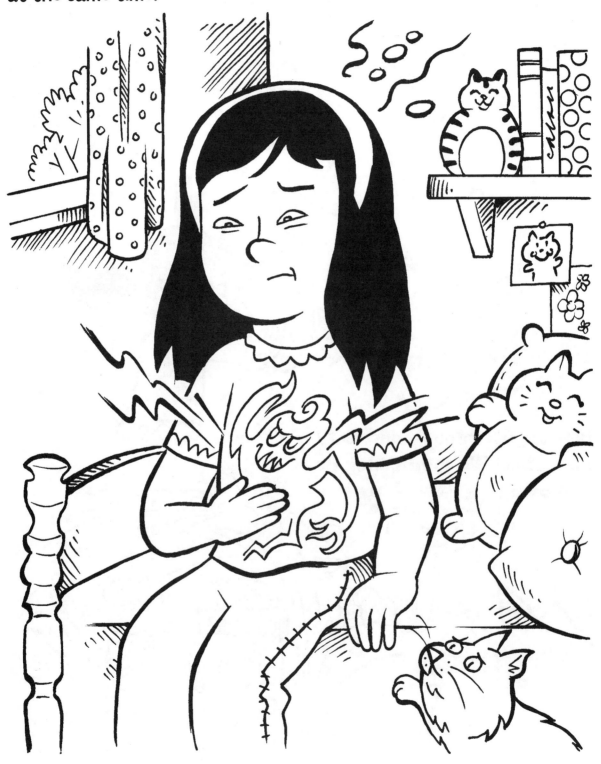

When Peter cut into line, how did William's anger leak out? Think back to the beginning of our story. Yes, you've got it! William's anger leaked out his hands when he pushed Peter, out his mouth when he yelled, and out his feet when he stormed away. When **you** get filled with Anger Squiggles, where do they leak out?

Poor William. He had no choice in the matter, did he? Don't you think the principal knows about Anger Squiggles and will let William off the hook? Don't be too sure about that! Each of us gets Anger Squiggles, but we usually kick them out before they fill us up. William didn't know how to get rid of those nasty Anger Squiggles and he is just going to have to suffer the consequences of his behavior: No recess for a whole week.

William Battles The Anger Squiggles © 2008 Mar✶co Products, Inc. 1.800.448.2197

To try to prevent this from happening again, Mr. Ortega asked William to meet with Mrs. Chase, who specializes in fighting Anger Squiggles. What type of person specializes in fighting Anger Squiggles? A warrior? A knight? Close, but not exactly. Mrs. Chase is the school counselor. She's a normal person just like you or me, but William likes to imagine her as a wise wizard with a swirling cape and a pointed hat.

Once William had spent his week of recesses in the school office, he went to visit Mrs. Chase. He wasn't sure she would really be able to help him, but he was willing to try anything. He sure didn't want to have to give up recess ever again.

Here's what Mrs. Chase taught William to do when battling Anger Squiggles:

Step 1: Learn what makes you angry.
When you do, you will know when an Anger Squiggle is trying to make your body its home. Pay close attention to how your body feels when Anger Squiggles are invading it. You might feel your face getting hot or you might start to shake or feel your fists clench.

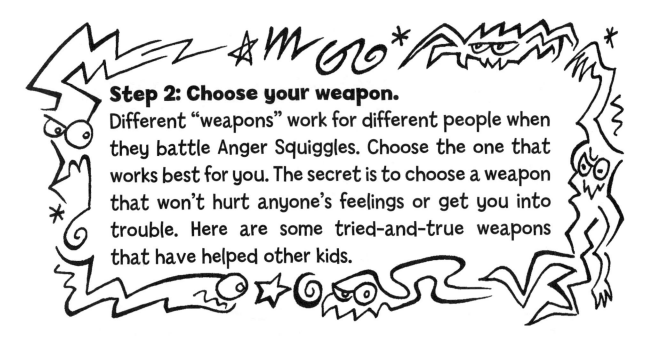

Step 2: Choose your weapon.

Different "weapons" work for different people when they battle Anger Squiggles. Choose the one that works best for you. The secret is to choose a weapon that won't hurt anyone's feelings or get you into trouble. Here are some tried-and-true weapons that have helped other kids.

#1. **Talk it out!** Tell someone that you're mad and tell him or her why. Watch those Anger Squiggles disappear.

#2. **Work it out!** Run fast, kick a ball, jump rope, or hit a tetherball. Your Anger Squiggles are no match for all of your positive energy. Watch those Squiggles drop, one by one, as you work it out.

#3. **Write it out!** Write what makes you angry in your journal and save it forever or scribble it on scratch paper and throw it away. Either way, you win. The more you write, the more quickly those Squiggles wither away.

Boys and girls, Anger Squiggles are no match for you! You will get angry. Everyone does. But remember: You can beat any Anger Squiggle, no matter how big and hairy it is! Just follow those two steps that Mrs. Chase taught William.

1. Recognize what makes you angry so you'll know when the Anger Squiggles are trying to take over.

2. Make sure that you don't get filled with Anger Squiggles and explode. Fight the Anger Squiggles with the "weapon" that works best for you.

Just two days after meeting with Mrs. Chase, William and his new battle plan were put to the test. Three things had happened, and he could feel the Anger Squiggles squirming around inside him. His sister ate all of the Fruit Flakes, Bettyanne called him "Short Stuff," and Johnny Waters laughed at him when he tripped in the hallway. William decided that he'd better battle the Anger Squiggles or risk losing control!

William thought about what Mrs. Chase had taught him. He could almost hear her whisper, "You know what has made you angry. Remember, William: "Talk it out." With that, William marched right up to his sister and said, "It makes me furious when you finish all the cereal before I have a chance to eat any!" As he spoke, William felt like a black belt ninja sneaking up and destroying that big, hairy Anger Squiggle his sister had caused.

William felt relieved, but he knew that two Anger Squiggles were still inside him. Then he heard Mrs. Chase's voice again. "Write it out, William." That is exactly what he did. He wrote all about how Johnny laughed at him in front of everyone. He wrote about how angry he was and how he wished he could go back and say something really mean to Johnny. By the time William finished writing about why he was angry, he felt like a Medieval knight riding in on a black stallion, using his sword to chop that spiky Anger Squiggle into bits.

William was feeling much better, but the last Anger Squiggle was still stuck inside him. Bettyanne was nowhere to be found, so William couldn't tell her how angry he was. His hand hurt, so he didn't want to write anything. William was about to give up his battle when he heard a voice whisper, "Work it out, William."

"That's it!" thought William. "I will work it out at recess."

William Battles The Anger Squiggles © 2008 Mar✳co Products, Inc. 1.800.448.2197

To destroy that final Anger Squiggle, William chose to play kickball, a game that allows kicking, throwing, and running. With each whack on the ball, William felt like a red-caped superhero using his X-ray vision to melt that long, skinny Anger Squiggle into a helpless puddle.

William Battles The Anger Squiggles © 2008 Mar✶co Products, Inc. 1.800.448.2197

William felt fantastic! He no longer worried about those nasty Anger Squiggles or about losing control. He knew that he would still get angry, but he was prepared. His battle plan was ready! Now go and prepare yours!

William Battles The Anger Squiggles

Student Booklet

Allow me to introduce William. He's an average kid, with average friends, who goes to an average school, and usually has pretty average days. But today will be different. Today will be anything but an average day.

Today William will **explode!**

What is the cause of this blow-up? Something so small that on an average day, William wouldn't give it a second thought. But we already know that today won't be like most days for William. We know that today will be different. So here is what finally pushed William over the edge: Peter Duncan cut in front of him in line at the drinking fountain.

What happened next shocked even William. His fists clenched into tight balls. His face felt hot and turned tomato red. William's hands developed a mind of their own and threw Peter to the ground. William heard himself scream, "Get out of my way!" He stormed away, but the principal's whistle stopped him in his tracks. Mr. Ortega had seen it all.

Anger Squiggles caused William to explode. Yes, Anger Squiggles ... Squiggles that grow and fill us up whenever we get angry. They are perfectly normal and they don't usually cause us too many problems. But there are days when Anger Squiggles get out of control. Do you know what happens then? Yes, you guessed it: We **EXPLODE**. Just like William did.

What happened earlier in the day that caused Anger Squiggles to take control of William? The first thing happened in the morning, when William was awakened by his teenage sister yelling, "You're late, Silly Willy." William hated being called "Silly Willy" and before he knew it, he had a short, fat Anger Squiggle inside him.

The story doesn't end here. William faced one frustrating situation after another. He missed breakfast and, instead of his favorite Sugary Snaps, William had dry toast. That brought one long, skinny Anger Squiggle into the picture.

In his dash to catch the bus, William left his homework on the kitchen table. Bing! Bing! A spiky, red-headed Anger Squiggle appeared as a result of that tragedy.

Finally on the bus, William discovered that the only seat left was between two girls from Grade 5. The rest of the kids hooted, whistled, and teased him. Because of that humiliation, a striped, fanged, hideous-looking Anger Squiggle and a brown, lumpy, three-horned Anger Squiggle grew inside William.

William was filling up with Anger Squiggles. There was hardly any room left in that body of his. If one more annoying thing happened, another Anger Squiggle would try to squeeze its way in, causing William to **EXPLODE**!

Let's get back to William as he patiently waits in line to use the drinking fountain. Remember: He has had a rotten day, and many different Anger Squiggles are swimming around inside him.

The tiny Anger Squiggle that arrived when Peter cut into line in front of William had nowhere to go. The other rotten Squiggles began to leak out to make room for it.

When Anger Squiggles start to leak out of our bodies, they do so in different ways.

They can leak out of our eyes,

our mouths,

Some Anger Squiggles leak into heads and tummies. Instead of causing you to hit, kick, or yell, these Squiggles cause you to feel really bad, giving you a headache or stomachache. Sometimes both at the same time!

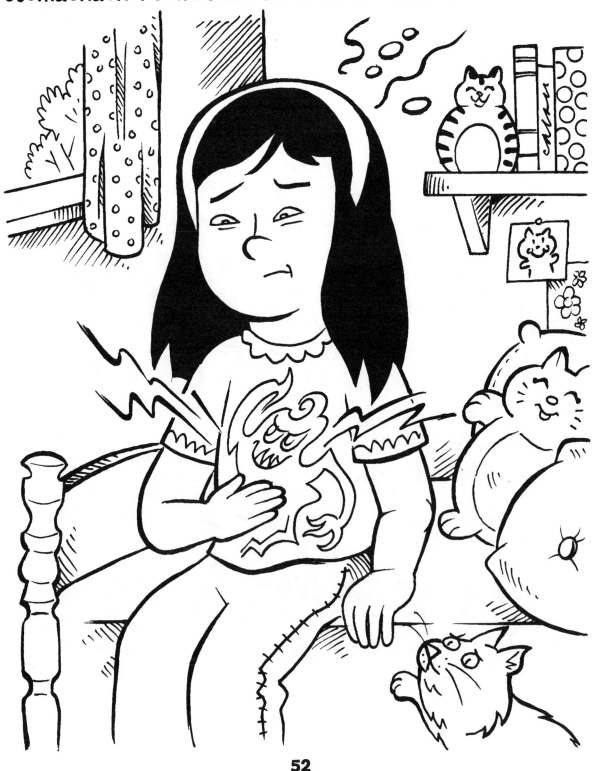

When Peter cut into line, how did William's anger leak out? It leaked out his hands when he pushed Peter, out his mouth when he yelled, and out his feet when he stormed away. When you get filled with Anger Squiggles, where do they leak out?

Poor William. He had no choice in the matter, right? Wrong! Each of us gets Anger Squiggles, but we usually kick them out before they fill us up. Because William didn't know how to do that, Mr. Ortega took away his recess for a whole week.

William Battles The Anger Squiggles © 2008 Mar∗co Products, Inc. 1.800.448.2197

To try to prevent this from happening again, Mr. Ortega asked William to meet with Mrs. Chase, who specializes in fighting Anger Squiggles. What type of person specializes in fighting Anger Squiggles? A warrior? A knight? Close, but not exactly. Mrs. Chase is the school counselor. William likes to imagine her as a wise wizard, complete with a cape and a pointed hat.

Once William had spent his week of recesses in the school office, he went to visit Mrs. Chase. He sure didn't want to have to give up recess ever again.

Here is what Mrs. Chase taught William to do when battling Anger Squiggles:

Step 1: Learn what makes you angry.
Pay close attention to how your body feels when Anger Squiggles are invading it.

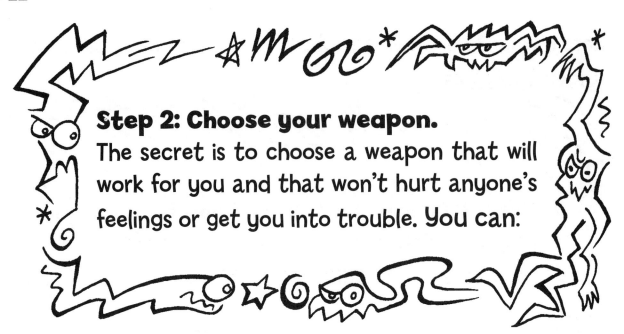

Step 2: Choose your weapon.
The secret is to choose a weapon that will work for you and that won't hurt anyone's feelings or get you into trouble. You can:

#1. **Talk it out!** Tell someone that you're mad and tell him or her and why.

#2. **Work it out!** Run fast, kick a ball, jump rope, or hit a tetherball. Your Anger Squiggles are no match for all of your positive energy.

#3. **Write it out!** Write what makes you angry in your journal and save it forever or scribble it on scratch paper and throw it away.

Boys and girls, Anger Squiggles are no match for you! You can beat any Anger Squiggle, no matter how big and hairy it is! Just follow these two steps that Mrs. Chase taught William.

1. Recognize what makes you angry so you'll know when the Anger Squiggles are trying to take over.

2. Make sure that you don't get filled with Anger Squiggles and explode. Fight the Anger Squiggles with the "weapon" that works best for you.

Just two days after meeting with Mrs. Chase, William and his new battle plan were put to the test. Three things happened, and he could feel the Anger Squiggles squirming around inside him. His sister ate all of the Fruit Flakes, Bettyanne called him "Short Stuff," and Johnny Waters laughed at him when he tripped in the hallway. William decided that he'd better battle the Anger Squiggles or risk losing control!

William thought about what Mrs. Chase had taught him: "Remember, William: Talk it out." With that, William marched right up to his sister and said, "It makes me furious when you finish all the cereal before I have a chance to eat any!" As he spoke, William felt like a black belt ninja sneaking up and destroying that big, hairy Anger Squiggle that his sister had caused.

William Battles The Anger Squiggles © 2008 Mar∗co Products, Inc. 1.800.448.2197

William felt relieved, but he knew that two Anger Squiggles remained inside him. Mrs. Chase's voice came to him again: "Write it out, William." That is exactly what he did. He wrote all about how Johnny laughed at him in front of everyone. He wrote about how angry he was and how he wished he could go back and say something really mean to Johnny. By the time William finished writing, he felt like a Medieval knight on a black stallion, using his sword to chop that spiky Anger Squiggle into bits.

William was feeling much better, but the last Anger Squiggle was stuck inside him. Bettyanne was nowhere to be found, so William couldn't tell her how angry he was. His hand hurt, so he didn't want to write anything. William was about to give up his battle when he heard a voice whisper, "Work it out, William."

"That's it!" thought William. "I will work it out at recess."

To destroy that final Anger Squiggle, William chose to play kickball, a game that allows kicking, throwing, and running. With each whack on the ball, William felt like a red-caped superhero using his X-ray vision to melt that long, skinny Anger Squiggle into a helpless puddle.

William felt fantastic! He no longer worried about those nasty Anger Squiggles or about losing control. He knew that he would still get angry, but he was prepared. His battle plan was ready! Now go and prepare yours!

Anger-Management Group Curriculum

Grades 3-6

Group Size: 4-8

Duration: 10 Weeks

SESSION 1
Introduction

Purpose:

To explain the group's parameters, establish rules, and begin to build group cohesion

Materials Needed:

For The Leader:

- ☐ *Facilitator Handout #1* (page 72)
- ☐ *Facilitator Handout #2* (page 73)
- ☐ 2 Large pieces of paper
- ☐ Tape
- ☐ Marker
- ☐ Chalkboard and chalk or chart paper and marker

For Each Student:

- ☐ Folder
- ☐ Pencil
- ☐ Crayons
- ☐ Piece of paper

Presentation Preparation:

Write *True* on one large piece of paper and tape it to one wall. Write *False* on another large piece of paper and tape it to the opposite wall. Reproduce *Facilitator Handout #1* and *Facilitator Handout #2* for the leader.

Lesson:

▷ Tell the students that they have joined this group to learn about *anger* and *conflict resolution.*

▷ Discuss/explore the meaning of *conflict resolution.* Suggest that conflict resolution is a method of resolving problems with others in a peaceful way.

▷ Discuss/explore *anger*. Emphasize that anger is not a bad emotion, but that what we do with our anger can sometimes be negative.

▷ Tell the students that everyone gets angry and that we all need to learn, at some point in our lives, how to control angry feelings.

▷ Lead a discussion on the importance of learning to control anger.

Talk about what would happen if an adult lost control of his/her temper at work, at home, with his/her spouse and kids, etc. Help the students reach a final conclusion (i.e., "An adult who lost his or her temper at work might hit someone. He or she would get fired, might get arrested, and then wouldn't have enough money to pay the bills.")

Ask the students what would happen to them if they lost control of their anger at school.

▷ Explain that in this group, the students will learn some "tricks" that will help them learn to control their anger and avoid the consequences of losing their temper.

▷ Discuss the group's parameters: frequency and duration of meetings, etc.

▷ Distribute a folder, crayons, and a pencil to each student and explain that the students will be getting some very special handouts to keep in these folders. Have each student write his/her name on the folder. (*Note:* If there is enough time at the end of the session, allow the students to decorate their folders. The facilitator should keep the folders and send them home with students after the final session.)

Group Rules:

▷ Have the students establish the group's rules and the consequences of breaking those rules. Write the rules on the board or chart paper.

▷ Some important rules that must be included:

One person talks at a time.
Respect confidentiality.
Show respect to others.

▷ Distribute a piece of paper to each student and have the students copy the rules and consequences from the board or chart paper, sign the rule sheet (showing their agreement to follow each rule), and place it in their folders.

Getting To Know You Activity:

▷ Show the students the two pieces of paper taped to the wall. One should read "True" and the other "False." Tell the students you're going to read a statement and that they should stand up and walk to the sign corresponding to their answer to that statement. When the next statement is read, the students should stay where they are or move to the other wall.

▷ Read the following statements:

This is my first year at this school.
I have played on a soccer team before.
I have played on a baseball team before.
I have slept in a tent.
I am the oldest in my family.
I am the youngest in my family.
I am a good dancer.
I can speak more than one language.
I like to play videogames.
Chocolate is my favorite flavor of ice cream.
I sing in the shower.
I was nervous about this group before today.

▷ If time permits, allow a few students to come up with their own statements and let the group respond to them.

Presentation—Numbers 0-10:

▷ Tell the students that you will begin each group session by asking each person to choose a number corresponding to how he/she feels.

▷ Show the students *Facilitator Handout #1*. As you explain the meaning of the different numbers, add your own illustrations so it looks similar to *Facilitator Handout #2*. (Handout #2 is only for the facilitator's reference at this point.)

▷ Explain that 10 and 0 are numbers that we don't use very often. They are for extreme days, when you feel really great and nothing could be better (10) or terrible days, when things couldn't get much worse (0).

▷ Discuss how our numbers usually fall between 1 and 9. 1 and 2 are for very sad or mad days, while 8 and 9 are for very good days, 5 is for days that are just OK, etc.

▷ Explain that someone's numbers may change throughout the day. A person may wake up late and feel a 4, for example, and that number may later grow to a 7 when he/she gets an *A* on a math test, to an 8 when a friend invites him/her over after school, and fall to a 5 when he/she isn't allowed to go to that friend's house.

▷ Ask each student his/her number and, if time permits, allow students who choose to do so to give brief explanations of their numbers. Write each student's name above the chosen number and on *Facilitator Handout #1*. Save the handout for future reference. During the following sessions, discuss the students' numbers, asking questions and prompting discussion. This gives the facilitator insight into each student's feelings.

▷ Congratulate the students on a job well done. Remind them when the group will meet again and discuss the proper procedure for returning to class, etc.

0 ---- 1 ---- 2 ---- 3 ---- 4 ---- 5 ---- 6 ---- 7 ---- 8 ---- 9 ---- 10

WEEK OF

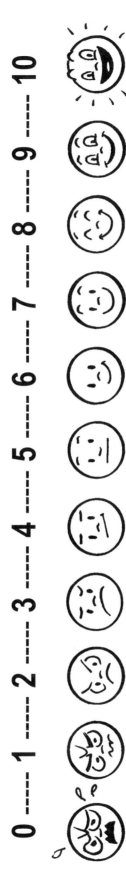

0 ---- 1 ---- 2 ---- 3 ---- 4 ---- 5 ---- 6 ---- 7 ---- 8 ---- 9 ---- 10

SESSION 2
Introduction To Anger

Purpose:

To introduce the concept of *anger* and how it builds inside each of us

Materials Needed:

For The Leader:

- ☐ *William Battles The Anger Squiggles Leader's Guide* (pages 1–10)
- ☐ Copy of *Facilitator Handout #2* (page 73)

For Each Student:

- ☐ Folder
- ☐ Copy of *William Battles The Anger Squiggles Student Booklet*
- ☐ Pencil
- ☐ Crayons or colored pencils
- ☐ Copy of *William Gets Filled With Anger Squiggles* (page 76)

Presentation Preparation:

Reproduce *William Battles The Anger Squiggles Student Booklet* and *William Gets Filled With Anger Squiggles* for each student. Reproduce *Facilitator Handout #2* for the leader.

Presentation—Numbers 0-10:

▷ Allow a different student to begin each session. As the students recite their numbers, try to paraphrase their meaning. (i.e., "You picked an 8. I think that means you're feeling pretty happy today. Is that right?" or "I see you picked a 2. That is a pretty low number. I'm guessing that you are feeling really angry or really sad or both.") Be careful never to make a declarative statement about a child's feelings. Always include a phrase like "Is that right?" or "I am guessing…" Record each student's answer above the number on *Facilitator Handout #2's* number line.

Lesson:

▷ Distribute a copy of *William Battles The Anger Squiggles Student Booklet,* a folder, a pencil, and crayons to each student.

▷ Read pages 1–10 of *William Battles The Anger Squiggles* from the *Leader's Guide.* Tell the students to follow along in their student booklets.

▷ After finishing page 10, facilitate discussion by asking such questions as, "Has anything like this ever happened to you?" or "How would you feel if you were William?"

▷ Distribute *William Gets Filled With Anger Squiggles* to each student. Instruct the students to draw, in William, their own Anger Squiggles. This will give them an opportunity to express how they imagine Anger Squiggles might look.

▷ Allow the students to complete their drawings and, if time allows, begin to color pages 1–10. When the allotted time has elapsed, ask the students to place their booklets and activity pages inside their folders.

▷ Collect the folders and any other distributed materials and save them for the next session.

▷ Conclude the session by asking the students to describe how they feel at this time by using the same numbering system they used at the beginning of the session. Record their answers next to the number given below the line. This will give the facilitator an opportunity to evaluate the students' feelings before and after the session.

▷ Thank the students for coming and remind them when the group will meet again.

75
William Battles The Anger Squiggles © 2008 Mar✶co Products, Inc. 1.800.448.2197

WILLIAM GETS FILLED WITH ANGER SQUIGGLES

Name_____

Recognizing How We Lose Control Of Our Anger

Purpose:

To help students, in a non-judgmental manner, identify the ways they lose control of their anger

Materials Needed:

For The Leader:

- ☐ *William Battles The Anger Squiggles Leader's Guide* (pages 11–17)
- ☐ Copy of *Facilitator Handout #2* (page 73)

For Each Student:

- ☐ Folder
- ☐ *William Battles The Anger Squiggles Student Booklet*
- ☐ Copy of *Anger Squiggles Can Leak Out* (page 79)
- ☐ Black crayon

Presentation Preparation:

Reproduce *Anger Squiggles Can Leak Out* for each student and *Facilitator's Handout #2* for the leader.

Presentation—Numbers 0-10:

▷ Allow a different student to begin this session. Ask each student for his/her current number, following the same procedure as in previous sessions. Record the students' answers on *Facilitator Handout #2*.

Lesson:

▷ Distribute the students' folders and black crayons.

▷ Briefly review the concepts presented in the last session, when the group discussed pages 1–10 of *William Battles The Anger Squiggles.*

▷ From the *Leader's Guide,* read pages 11–13 of *William Battles The Anger Squiggles.* Tell the students to follow along in their student booklets.

▷ After you read page 13, have the students close their booklets so they cannot see the illustrations on pages 14 and 15.

▷ Read pages 14 and 15, asking all four of the questions listed on pages. Allow the students to answer.

▷ Have the students open their booklets to pages 14 and 15. Review the ways anger can leak out.

▷ Continue reading pages 16 and 17 of the story. Allow for a few minutes of discussion.

▷ Distribute *Anger Squiggles Can Leak Out.* Review the sentence to be completed and give the following example: "When I allow myself to get filled up with Anger Squiggles, they leak out through my eyes and I cry, my feet and I kick, and my mouth and I say bad words." Ask the students to mark in black the areas of their body from which their anger leaks out. For example, a student who hits when he/she is angry would color his/her hands. Once the students have completed the handout, have them share and explain their drawings.

▷ Tell the students to look at page 17 in their booklet, as they say, "This is a picture of me. (Students should point to the picture that matches what they do.) When I get filled with Anger Squiggles, they leak out of my (NAME THE PART OF THE BODY) and I (NAME THE ACTION).

▷ If time allows, the students may continue coloring in their booklets, but not going past page 17. When the allotted time has elapsed, ask them to place their booklets and activity page inside their folders.

▷ Collect the folders and any other distributed materials and save them for the next session.

▷ Conclude the session by asking the students to identify how they feel at this time by using the same numbering system they used at the beginning of the lesson. Record their answers beside the number given below the line.

▷ Thank the students for coming and remind them when the group will meet again.

ANGER SQUIGGLES CAN LEAK OUT

Name_____

Directions: Think about *your* Anger Squiggles and the parts of your body they affect. Complete the sentence below, then mark in black the areas of your body where anger leaks out.

When I allow myself to get filled with Anger Squiggles, they leak out through

my _____ and I _____,

my _____ and I _____,

and my _____ and I _____.

SESSION 4
Recognizing Body Cues For Angry Feelings

Purpose:

To give students a tangible way to recognize their angry feelings before they are overcome with emotion

Materials Needed:

For The Leader:

- ☐ *William And The Anger Squiggles Leader's Guide* (pages 18-20)
- ☐ 3 Baskets or large containers
- ☐ 3 Different-colored posterboards
- ☐ Marker
- ☐ Scrap paper or small ball
- ☐ Copy of *Facilitator Handout #2* (page 73)

For Each Student:

- ☐ Folder
- ☐ *William Battles The Anger Squiggles Student Booklet*
- ☐ Red marker
- ☐ Pencil
- ☐ Copy of *Where My Body Feels Anger* (page 83)

Presentation Preparation:

Identify each basket by the color of one of the posterboards. On three separate posterboards of corresponding colors, write:

"What makes people angry at school?"
"What makes people angry at home?"
"Say anything!"

If you're using scrap paper, wad it into a small ball. Reproduce *Where My Body Feels Anger* for each student and *Facilitator Handout #2* for the leader.

Presentation—Numbers 0-10:

▷ Allow a different student to begin this session. Ask each student for his/her current number, following the same procedure as in previous sessions. Record the students' answers on *Facilitator Handout #2*. Try to build group cohesion by recognizing any low numbers and by encouraging group members to give a little extra encouragement to anyone who has a low number.

Lesson:

▷ Distribute the students' folders.

▷ Briefly review the concepts covered in pages 1–17 of *William Battles The Anger Squiggles.*

▷ Read pages 18-20 in *William Battles The Anger Squiggles* while the students follow along with the student booklets.

▷ Distribute *Where My Body Feels Anger,* a pencil, and a red marker to each student. Review the sentence to be completed and give the following example: "I can tell when Anger Squiggles are trying to make my body their home by paying close attention to my body's clues. The hints my body gives me are: My fists clench, my face turns red, and my stomach hurts."

▷ Have the students use the red marker to color the areas of their bodies where they first feel their anger. Have them complete the sentence on the activity page.

▷ Each student should then present his/her drawing and explain it to the group.

▷ Any students who finish before the allotted time has elapsed should be allowed to color pages in their student booklets without going past page 20. When the allotted time has elapsed, ask the students to place their booklets and activity pages inside their folders.

▷ Collect the folders and any other distributed materials and save them for the next session.

Activity:

▷ Involve the students in *What Makes You Angry?* This activity may be adapted to fit many different games.

▷ Place the baskets and their corresponding posters at a suitable distance from the students.

▷ Tell the students to throw the ball toward the baskets. A student whose ball lands in a basket must answer the question written on the corresponding posterboard. "Say anything" is an opportunity for the students to share any appropriate personal information they think would be of interest to the group.

▷ Begin the game and write each student's answer on its corresponding posterboard.

▷ Conclude the session by asking the students to describe how they feel by using the same numbering system they used at the beginning of the lesson. Record their answers beside the number given below the line.

▷ Recognize the students' hard work and remind them when the group will meet again.

WHERE MY BODY FEELS ANGER

Name_____

Directions: Think about *your* Anger Squiggles and the parts of your body they affect. Complete the sentence below, then mark in red the areas of your body where you first feel anger.

I can tell that Anger Squiggles are trying to make my body their home by paying close attention to my body's clues. The hints my body gives me are

_____ , _____

and _____ .

SESSION 5
Dealing Effectively With Anger

Purpose:

To help students learn various ways of effectively dealing with anger and provide each student with the opportunity to think about which method best suits his/her personality

Materials Needed:

For The Leader:

☐ *William Battles The Anger Squiggles Leader Guide* (pages 21-30)
☐ Copy of *Facilitator Handout #2* (page 73)

For Each Student:

☐ Folder
☐ *William Battles The Anger Squiggles Student Booklet*
☐ Copy of *Ways To Battle Anger Squiggles* (page 86)
☐ Crayons or colored pencils
☐ Drawing paper
☐ Pencil

Presentation Preparation

Reproduce *Ways To Battle Anger Squiggles* for each student and *Facilitator Handout #2* for the leader.

Presentation—Numbers 0-0:

▷ Allow a different student to begin this session. Ask each student for his/her current number, following the same procedure as in previous sessions. Record the students' answers on *Facilitator Handout #2*.

Lesson:

▷ Briefly review pages 1–20 of *William Battles The Anger Squiggles*.

▷ Read pages 21-23 in *William Battles The Anger Squiggles Leader's Guide* while the students follow along with the student booklets.

▷ Lead a discussion on other ways to fight Anger Squiggles. Include such things as playing soccer, talking calmly to myself, reading a book, thinking about a happy memory, etc.

▷ Distribute the students' folders. Distribute *Ways To Battle Anger Squiggles* and a pencil to each student.

▷ Review the ideas mentioned on *Ways To Battle Anger Squiggles*. Have the students write or draw other ideas in the three remaining boxes. When everyone has finished, have the students share their answers with the group, then place their handouts in their folders.

▷ Continue by reading pages 24-30 of *William Battles The Anger Squiggles* while the students follow along in their booklets.

▷ Discuss the end of the story. Explore the idea that William continued to get angry, but was proactive in battling the Anger Squiggles.

Activity:

▷ Distribute drawing paper and colored pencils or crayons and allow the students to draw the ways they will get rid of their own Anger Squiggles.

▷ Allow time for the students to share their drawings with the group.

▷ When everyone has finished, have the students put their drawings and their booklets into their folders.

▷ Collect the students' folders and any other distributed materials.

▷ Conclude the session by asking the students to describe how they are feeling, using the same numbering system they used at the beginning of the session. Record their answers beside the number given below the line.

▷ Congratulate the students on their hard work and remind them when you will see them next.

William Battles The Anger Squiggles © 2008 Mar★co Products, Inc. 1.800.448.2197

WAYS TO BATTLE ANGER SQUIGGLES

Name_____

Directions: Three ways to battle Anger Squiggles are shown below. In the empty boxes, write and/or draw three other ways you could battle your Anger Squiggles.

Work It Out	Write It Out
Talk It Out	

SESSION 6
Learning To Talk It Out

Purpose:

To introduce the idea of *non-verbal communication* and help students learn to better express themselves by matching non-verbal communication with verbal communication

Materials Needed:

For The Leader:

- ☐ Copy of *Facilitator Handout #2* (page 73)
- ☐ Copy of *Facilitator Handout #3* (page 89)
- ☐ Cup
- ☐ Scissors
- ☐ Chalkboard and chalk or chart paper and marker

For Each Student: None

Presentation Preparation:

Reproduce *Facilitator Handout #2* for the leader. Reproduce *Facilitator Handout #3,* cut the strips apart, fold them, and place each one in the cup.

Presentation—Numbers 0- 10:

▷ Discuss how "feelings numbers" can change throughout the day. Ask for volunteers to discuss the different numbers they have had during the day. Then allow a different student to begin the session, following the same procedure as in previous sessions and recording the students' answers on *Facilitator Handout #2.*

Lesson:

▷ Explain the meanings of and differences between *verbal* and *non-verbal communication.* Explain that *words* are verbal communication and *posture, tone of voice,* and *eye contact* are non-verbal means of communicating.

▷ Explain to the students that the messages they send through non-verbal communication are often more powerful than the words they speak.

▷ Illustrate this point by giving an example. Say, "I am really excited to play with you!" in a negative tone, with an angry affect. Discuss how tone of voice influences what is heard.

▷ On the chalkboard or chart paper, list various examples of non-verbal communication. Your list should include: posture, tone of voice, amount of eye contact, mannerisms, and anything else you feel is appropriate. When the list is complete, review each item and explain how it affects communication. For example, you might say, "I really want to play soccer," in a not-too-excited voice while shrugging your shoulders.

Activity:

▷ Have each student draw one strip of paper from the cup and read the printed statement as if he/she is happy, worried, or angry. The students should use verbal and non-verbal communications skills. Discuss how the group can tell which emotion each student represents. Continue the activity for as long as time permits.

▷ Review the idea that although we communicate in many different ways, non-verbal messages are often the most powerful. That's why it is important that we recognize the messages we convey through body language as well as through words.

▷ Conclude the session by asking the students to describe how they are feeling, using the same numbering system they used at the beginning of the session. Record their answers beside the number given below the line.

▷ Remind the students when you will see them next and that only four group sessions remain. (This will allow for proper termination.)

88

Are you coming to my birthday party?
I was sitting there first.
You took the pencil I was using.
Do you want to be my partner?
I want to go first.
We're in the same group.
I will be moving at the end of the year.
I am going to be the duck in the play.
Where are you going?
You are so funny.
What's wrong?
Look where you're going.
I am glad that we're partners.
I have to go to soccer practice after school.
George and Tony are coming with us.
Hurry up! It's time to go.
This is what you got for your birthday?

SESSION 7
Talking It Out: Assertiveness Skills

Purpose:

To introduce the idea of being *assertive* rather than being *aggressive* or *passive* and to explore the benefits of assertiveness and the pitfalls of being passive or aggressive

Materials Needed:

For The Leader:

☐ Copy of *Facilitator Handout #2* (page 73)

For Each Student:

☐ Folder
☐ Copy of *Rabbits, Horses, And Crocodiles* (page 92)
☐ Copy of *The Horse, The Crocodile, The Rabbit, And The Chicken* (pages 93-95)
☐ Corresponding puppets or stuffed animals to be used in the puppet show (Animals in the puppet show may be changed to fit the type of puppets available.)

Presentation Preparation

Reproduce *Rabbits, Horses, And Crocodiles* and *The Horse, The Crocodile, The Rabbit, And The Chicken* for each student. Obtain puppets or stuffed animals to be used in the puppet show. Reproduce *Facilitator Handout #2* for the leader.

Presentation—Numbers 0-10:

▷ Ask for volunteers to describe a time during the past week when they felt a 9. Then ask each student for his/her current number, following the same procedure as in previous sessions. Record the students' answers on *Facilitator Handout #2*.

Lesson:

▷ Distribute his/her folder and a copy of *Rabbits, Horses, And Crocodiles* to each student. Introduce the words *assertive, aggressive,* and *passive* by quickly reviewing the text on the handout.

▷ Distribute copies of *The Horse, The Crocodile, The Rabbit, And The Chicken* and assign puppet-play roles.

▷ Review the correct affect and tone for each character, based on the text in *Rabbits, Horses, And Crocodiles.*

Activity:

▷ Distribute the puppets to the students portraying the characters. Perform the puppet show.

▷ Then ask such open-ended questions as:

1. Why wasn't Rabbit asked to play? *(Rabbit was not friendly, and Chicken thought he did not want to play.)*

2. Why wasn't Crocodile asked to play? *(Crocodile was too aggressive. Chicken didn't want to be around her.)*

3. What did Horse do that made others want to be his friends? *(He was confident, friendly, and upbeat. He stood up for himself in a respectful way.)*

4. Which animal are you most like? *(Accept any appropriate answers, but have the students give the reasons for their choices. Thank the students for their honesty and willingness to share.)*

5. Would you like to change that? *(Accept any appropriate answers. Thank the students for their honesty and willingness to share.)*

6. How would you need to change to become more like Horse? *(Accept any appropriate answers.)*

▷ Conclude the session by asking the students to identify how they feel at this time by using the same numbering system they used at the beginning of the lesson. Record their answers beside the number given below the line.

▷ Have the students put their papers into their folders. Collect the students' folders. Remind the students when you will see them next and that only three group sessions remain.

RABBITS, HORSES, AND CROCODILES

Rabbits: Rabbits are passive.

- Rabbits don't tell people how they feel or say what they want.

- Rabbits are quiet, shy, and sometimes afraid.

- Sometimes rabbits get picked on because they don't stand up for themselves.

- Sometimes rabbits act like everything is OK even though they are really mad or sad.

- When rabbits are nervous, they often look at the ground, speak quietly, or stutter and don't get to the point.

- Sometimes rabbits have a hard time making friends because others can't tell if they want to be friends.

Crocodiles: Crocodiles are aggressive.

- Crocodiles can be loud and bossy and are often seen as bullies.

- Most others do not want to be a crocodile's friend.

- Crocodiles get angry very quickly and seem to be angry most of the time.

- When crocodiles are upset, they often stand too close to others and speak too loudly.

- Crocodiles may say what they want, but the disrespectful way they say it pushes others away from them.

Horses: Horses are assertive.

- Horses look others in the eyes, but stand a comfortable distance away.

- Horses have many friends, because they stand up for themselves but don't bully others.

- Horses tell others what they want in a respectful tone. They don't keep their feelings inside.

- Horses have a positive attitude.

THE HORSE, THE CROCODILE, THE RABBIT, AND THE CHICKEN

Narrator #1:

This story is about four very different animals. The first animal is Passive Rabbit, and he is very scared and shy. When Passive Rabbit wants something, he never feels comfortable asking for it. He tries to hint at what he wants, and others don't usually know what he is trying to say. Many have learned that they can treat Passive Rabbit badly because he won't stand up for himself. He gets picked on a lot.

Narrator #2:

The second animal is Aggressive Crocodile, who is grumpy, loud, and rude. When Aggressive Crocodile wants something, she demands it. She calls people names, bosses them around, and acts like a big bully. Aggressive Crocodile frightens others, and most don't want to be her friend.

Narrator #3:

The third animal is Assertive Horse, who is pretty easygoing. He isn't scared of others, but he never bosses others around. When Assertive Horse wants something, he usually asks for it in a nice, polite way. Others like to hang around Assertive Horse because he never makes fun of them and he is a good, trustworthy friend. But he won't let anyone walk all over him! He stands up for himself in a way that doesn't break any rules.

Narrator #1:

The fourth animal in this story is Chatty Chicken, who lives in the same neighborhood. Chatty Chicken's parents, Mom and Dad Chicken, recently gave her a new videogame. All the animals in the neighborhood heard about Chatty Chicken's new game. They were anxious to play the game, and Chatty Chicken was excited to show it to everyone.

When Chatty Chicken was walking to the park one day, she saw Passive Rabbit.

William Battles The Anger Squiggles © 2008 Mar∗co Products, Inc. 1.800.448.2197

CHICKEN: "Hey, Passive Rabbit!"

RABBIT: "Ohhh, Hi, Chatty Chicken."

CHICKEN: "What have you been up to, Passive Rabbit?"

RABBIT: "Ohhh … I don't … know … Nothing, I guess."

CHICKEN: "Well, I got a new videogame and it's great!"

RABBIT: "Ohhh … yeah … I heard."

Narrator #2:

Passive Rabbit was silently wishing that Chatty Chicken would see how much he wanted to come over and play. But he was too shy to say anything about it.

CHICKEN: "Yes, and my parents said I could invite a friend over to play."

RABBIT: "Hmmmm … That sounds nice."

CHICKEN: "Yeah, it is. As a matter of fact, I am going to play right now."

Narrator #3:

Chatty Chicken walked away, thinking that Passive Rabbit didn't sound interested in playing with her. Passive Rabbit pouted because Chatty Chicken never invited him to play the new game. On her way home, Chatty Chicken ran into Aggressive Crocodile.

CROCODILE: "Hey, Chatty Chicken! I heard you got a new videogame."

CHICKEN: "Yep!"

CROCODILE: "Well, give it to me!"

CHICKEN: "Are you kidding me? I am not giving my game to anyone."

CROCODILE: "Then LET ME PLAY IT!"

William Battles The Anger Squiggles © 2008 Mar*co Products, Inc. 1.800.448.2197

Narrator #1:

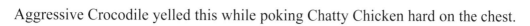

Aggressive Crocodile yelled this while poking Chatty Chicken hard on the chest.

CROCODILE: "You will be sorry if you don't let me play with your new game!"

CHICKEN: "What are you talking about, Aggressive Crocodile?"

CROCODILE: "I'm just saying that if you know what's good for you, you'll give me the game. Or at least let me play it for a while!"

CHICKEN: "Get lost, Aggressive Crocodile! You're so bossy! Can't you see why the other animals don't want to play with you?"

Narrator #2:

Chatty Chicken walked away while Aggressive Crocodile angrily kicked a wall because she had lost her chance to play the new videogame. Just when Chatty Chicken thought she would never find anyone to play with, she ran into Assertive Horse.

CHICKEN: "Hey, Horse! How are you doing?"

HORSE: "Good!"

CHICKEN: "Did you hear that I got a new videogame?"

HORSE: "Yeah! I heard it's awesome, too!"

CHICKEN: "It is."

HORSE: "Well, do you think I could come check it out? I have always wanted to see that game"

CHICKEN: "Sure! I was starting to think I would never find anyone to play with. I can show you how to play, then we can challenge each other."

HORSE: "Sounds good. Let's go!"

William Battles The Anger Squiggles © 2008 Mar✶co Products, Inc. 1.800.448.2197

SESSION 8
More Assertiveness Skills

Purpose:

To teach students four simple steps for becoming assertive

Materials Needed:

For The Leader:

- ☐ Copy of *Facilitator Handout #2* (page 73)
- ☐ Copy of *Facilitator Handout #4* (pages 99-101)
- ☐ 4 Pieces of posterboard or whiteboard
- ☐ Marker
- ☐ Scissors
- ☐ Container

For Each Student:

- ☐ Folder
- ☐ Copy of *Rabbits, Horses, And Crocodiles* (from Session 7)

Presentation Preparation:

Using the marker, write the *Four Steps To Acting Assertively* on the posterboard/white board. Use one piece of posterboard/whiteboard for each step.

Step 1: Speak with the other person in private.

Step 2: Look and sound assertive.

Step 3: Use the "assertive sentences."

I _____ when _____.
    (I don't like it/ I feel bad, sad, etc.)   (you tease me, I get called names, etc.)

I would appreciate it if _____.
                      (you would stop.)

Step 4: Add something positive and true.

1. "You seem fun. Maybe we can be friends some day."
2. "I notice that you like to play basketball. If we can solve this problem, I would really like to play basketball with you some day."
3. "We were friends before, and I would really like it if we could be friends again."
4. "I would really like to get to know you. Maybe we could be friends some day."

Reproduce *Facilitator Handout #2* for the leader. Reproduce *Facilitator Handout #4,* cut it into strips, and place the strips in the container.

Presentation—Numbers 0-10:

▷ Allow a different student to begin this session. Ask each student for his/her current number, following the same procedure as in previous sessions. Record the students' answers on *Facilitator Handout #2.* Encourage the group to offer support to any member with a low number.

Lesson:

▷ Review the puppet-show behaviors of the rabbit, crocodile, and horse. Emphasize the horse's behaviors.

▷ Distribute the students' folders.

▷ Using the Session 7 activity sheet *Rabbits, Horses, And Crocodiles*, create a list of assertive behaviors. The list should include *making good eye contact; standing still; using a calm, strong voice; etc.*

▷ Tell the students that the day's lesson is about learning to act more like Assertive Horse, which means standing up for themselves and saying what they want without being disrespectful or doing something that would get them into trouble.

▷ Introduce the *Four Steps To Acting Assertively* written on the posterboards. As you review the steps, tell the students to:

Step 1: Speak with the other person in private.
(Tell the students that when they have a concern, they should approach the person when no one is around or ask to speak with him/her in private. Discuss, as a group, why it would be important to do this.)

97

Step 2: Look and sound assertive.
(Refer to your list of assertive behaviors to reinforce this step.)

Step 3: Use the "assertive sentences."
(Tell the students to make sure what they're asking for is clear and measurable. "I would appreciate it if you'd stop calling me names" is better than "I would appreciate it if you'd stop being mean to me.")

Step 4: Add something positive and true.
(Review the sentences with the group. If this is too advanced for some students, simply skip this step.)

Activity:

▷ Have each student draw a description of a scenario from the container. The facilitator should also draw a scenario description from the container.

▷ Tell the students they are to respond to the scenario in an assertive way, following each of the four steps.

▷ Allow the students to look at the posterboards listing the four steps. Remind the students that assertive communication can be non-verbal as well as verbal.

▷ Begin the role-plays. The facilitator should go first, in order to show the students what they are to do. (*Note:* Students should not act out the background information. They should act out only the role-play.)

▷ Conclude the session by asking the students to identify how they feel at this time by using the same numbering system they used at the beginning of the lesson. Record their answers beside the number given below the line.

▷ Collect the students' folders. Remind the students when you will see them next and that only two group sessions remain.

*(Students should **not** act out the background information. They should act out only the role-play.)*

BACKGROUND INFORMATION: A student stands with a group of friends and whispers, points, and laughs every time you walk by.

ROLE-PLAY: Act out how you would approach the student and behave assertively. Remember: Make sure you are calm, speak with the person in private, and use assertive sentences.

BACKGROUND INFORMATION: A classmate asks you for your snack every day. When you refuse to give it to him, he threatens to tell every kid in the class not to be your friend. You're afraid that this student will turn the class against you, so you give him your snack.

ROLE-PLAY: Act out how you would approach the student and behave assertively. Remember: Make sure you are calm, speak with the person in private, and use assertive sentences.

BACKGROUND INFORMATION: A student who sits three rows behind you on the bus throws paper wads at you every day. When you turn around, kids are giggling and acting like they have no idea who threw the paper. You know exactly who threw it.

ROLE-PLAY: Act out how you would approach the student and behave assertively. Remember: Make sure you are calm, speak with the person in private, and use assertive sentences.

BACKGROUND INFORMATION: Two kids in your class whisper and giggle every time you answer a question the teacher asks. You can't hear what they're saying, but knowing that they're making fun of you hurts your feelings.

ROLE-PLAY: Act out how you would approach the students and behave assertively. Remember: Make sure you are calm, speak with them in private, and use assertive sentences.

BACKGROUND INFORMATION: During a basketball game, a student slams into you extra-hard. He does it every time you play basketball, but only when the teacher is not looking.

ROLE-PLAY: Act out how you would approach the student and behave assertively. Remember: Make sure you are calm, speak with the person in private, and use assertive sentences.

BACKGROUND INFORMATION: An older student tells other kids not to be friends with you because you are "not cool." You spend recess alone while the other kids play together.

ROLE-PLAY: Act out how you would approach the student and behave assertively. Remember: Make sure you are calm, speak with the person in private, and use assertive sentences.

BACKGROUND INFORMATION: One day at lunch, you approach a table where students from your class are sitting. When you try to sit down, a girl says, "Sorry, we don't have room for dorks." The rest of the kids giggle. You thought most of the kids at the table were your friends, but now you are not so sure.

ROLE-PLAY: Act out how you would approach the student and behave assertively. Remember: Make sure you are calm, speak with the person in private, and use assertive sentences.

BACKGROUND INFORMATION: A student has been telling other kids not to hang out with you because you are a trouble-maker. You are not a trouble-maker. Even if you were, you wouldn't want people saying that others shouldn't be your friends.

ROLE-PLAY: Act out how you would approach the student and behave assertively. Remember: Make sure you are calm, speak with the person in private, and use assertive sentences.

BACKGROUND INFORMATION: During gym class, a student kicks the ball at you extra-hard. He always plays very rough and calls you a baby and laughs at you when you ask him to stop it.

ROLE-PLAY: Act out how you would approach the student and behave assertively. Remember: Make sure you are calm, speak with the person in private, and use assertive sentences.

BACKGROUND INFORMATION: A student bumps into you in the hallway every day. She always apologizes in a fake way and tries to pretend that she didn't mean to bump into you. You can tell that it wasn't an accident.

ROLE-PLAY: Act out how you would approach the student and behave assertively. Remember: Make sure you are calm, speak with the person in private, and use assertive sentences.

SESSION 9
Review/Wrap-up

Purpose:

To reinforce the *Four Steps To Acting Assertively* as well as to review all eight previous sessions

Materials Needed:

For The Leader:

☐ Copy of *Facilitator Handout #2* (page 73)
☐ Scenario strips from Session 8
☐ Container
☐ *Four Steps To Acting Assertively* posters from Session 8

For Each Student:

☐ Folder

Presentation Preparation:

Place the scenario strips in the container. Turn the posters to the wall so the students cannot see what's written on them. Reproduce *Facilitator Handout #2* for the leader.

Presentation—Numbers 0-10:

▷ Ask for volunteers to describe a time during the previous week when they felt a 1 or a 2. Then ask each student for his/her current number, following the same procedure as in previous sessions. Record the students' answers on *Facilitator Handout #2.*

Lesson:

▷ Ask the students to recite the *Four Steps To Acting Assertively*. Keep the posters turned to the wall in order to test the group members' memories. If it seems necessary to show the students the posters in order to complete the task, turn them around so they can be seen.

Activity:

▷ Tell the students they will each have another opportunity to role-play. Have each student draw a scenario description from the container, making sure that he/she does not draw the same description as he/she did in Session 8. If the group members recall the *Four Steps To Acting Assertively*, turn the posterboards around to face the wall.

▷ Begin the role-plays, recognizing the assertive behaviors the students choose to use in their dramatizations.

▷ Distribute the students' folders.

▷ Explain that as a part of the last session, the students will be playing a game to see how much they have learned. In order for them to do well at the game, they will need to take a few minutes to review the material in their folders.

▷ Review each handout and allow different group members to summarize the lessons.

▷ Highlight the key points of each lesson.

▷ Conclude the session by asking the students to identify how they feel at this time by using the same numbering system they used at the beginning of the lesson. Record their answers beside the number given below the line.

▷ Collect the students' folders. Thank the students for participating. Remind them the next session will be the last session.

SESSION 10
Celebration

Purpose:

To review the curriculum as well as to celebrate what the group has accomplished (This allows for proper termination.)

Materials Needed:

For The Leader:

- ☐ Copy of *Facilitator Handout #2* (page 73)
- ☐ Copy of *Facilitator Handout #5* (pages 106-111)
- ☐ Die
- ☐ Small reward for each member (pencil, sticker, etc)
- ☐ Healthy treats (optional)

For Each Student:

- ☐ Folder

Presentation Preparation:

Reproduce *Facilitator Handout #2* for the leader. Reproduce *Facilitator Handout #5*. Cut apart the cards, then number the back of the cards as follows:

#1	General Questions
#2	Questions About You
#3	Role-Plays
#4	General Questions
#5	Getting To Know You Better
#6	Your Turn!

Stack the cards according to the number on the back of each card.

Optional: Create a party atmosphere by bringing healthy treats to enjoy throughout the session.

Presentation—Numbers 0-10:

▷ Allow a different student to begin this session. Ask each student for his/her current number, following the same procedure as in previous sessions and recording the students' answers on *Facilitator Handout #2.*

Lesson:

▷ Tell the students that during this last session, they will play a game that lets them answer questions about many different things. They may also perform role-plays. Everything they do will have something to do with what they have learned the weeks they have spent together in group.

Activity:

▷ Explain the following directions:

Each member will roll the die and draw from the stack a card whose number matches the number rolled on the die.

Some stacks include role-play scenarios, while others include questions to be answered.

Students will play as one team, but each student will have a turn to draw, read, answer a question, or perform a role-play.

Team members may confer before a student gives an answer.

▷ If giving a small prize to the group, tell the students what goal they must reach to earn the prize. (Make the goal attainable.)

▷ Conclude the session by asking the students to identify how they feel at this time by using the same numbering system they used at the beginning of the lesson. Record their answers beside the number given below the line.

▷ Congratulate the students on all they have learned. Distribute the students' folders, which they may take with them.

William Battles The Anger Squiggles © 2008 Mar✱co Products, Inc. 1.800.448.2197

General Questions

Describe an Anger Squiggle.

General Questions

Describe what happens if we allow ourselves to get filled up with Anger Squiggles.

General Questions

What three weapons did William use to battle his Anger Squiggles?

General Questions

Why is it important to listen to your body's clues that an Anger Squiggle is trying to move in?

General Questions

When choosing your weapon, make sure to choose one that won't _____ or _____.

General Questions

What are some different ways to "Work it out"?

Questions About You

What is the last thing that gave you an Anger Squiggle?

Questions About You

What types of things that happen at home give you Anger Squiggles?

Questions About You

What types of things that happen at school give you Anger Squiggles?

Questions About You

What types of things that happen with your friends give you Anger Squiggles?

Questions About You

How do you battle your Anger Squiggles?

Questions About You

When you allow yourself to get filled up with Anger Squiggles, where do they leak out?

Role-Plays

Using non-verbal communication, let someone know, "I am so happy that you are here" in a sarcastic manner, a friendly manner, and a disappointed manner. Allow the group to guess the feeling you are acting out.

Role-Plays

Act out your favorite way to battle Anger Squiggles. We will guess what it is!

Role-Plays

Act out an assertive way of responding to a person who just took the chair you were sitting in. Remember to use assertive sentences.

Role-Plays

Act out your favorite way to battle Anger Squiggles. We will guess what it is!

Role-Plays

Act out an assertive way of responding to a person who just bumped into you. Remember to use assertive sentences.

Role-Plays

Act out your favorite way to battle Anger Squiggles. We will guess what it is!

General Questions Describe a passive person.	**General Questions** Describe an assertive person.
General Questions Describe an aggressive person.	**General Questions** Why is it important to speak in private when being assertive?
General Questions Give an example of an assertive sentence.	**General Questions** In the puppet show, why did Chatty Chicken choose to play with Assertive Horse instead of Passive Rabbit or Aggressive Crocodile?

Getting To Know You Better

If you could go anywhere
on vacation, where would
you go?

Getting To Know You Better

What do you like to
do most on the weekend?

Getting To Know You Better

If you were president,
what laws would you change?

Getting To Know You Better

Do you have any pets?
What kind?

Getting To Know You Better

What is your favorite
subject in school? Why?

Getting To Know You Better

What is your favorite movie?
Why?

William Battles The Anger Squiggles © 2008 Mar∗co Products, Inc. 1.800.448.2197

Your Turn!

Tell us something about yourself that you would like the group to know.

Your Turn!

Name one thing you have learned about a group member as a result of being in this group.

Your Turn!

Roll again!

Your Turn!

Give someone in the group a compliment.

Your Turn!

Ask anyone in the group a question.

Your Turn!

What is the most important thing you have learned about yourself as a result of being in this group?

Katherine MacLeod

Katherine MacLeod attended the University of California, Santa Barbara, where she received her Bachelor of Arts degree in both Cultural Anthropology and Spanish. She later attended San Diego State University, where she earned her Master's degree in Social Work with an emphasis in Educational Social Work.

Katherine has worked as a school social worker and a school counselor in many diverse settings. She has successfully utilized her anger-management curriculum with students at the elementary and secondary levels. Katherine is currently working as an elementary school counselor in beautiful southern California.

In her free time, Katherine enjoys freelance photography, travel, and spending time with her husband Dave and her son William, to whom this book is dedicated.